# Color Your Own
# *Great Flower Prints*

*Gary Olson*

Charlene Tarbox

## DOVER PUBLICATIONS, INC.
Mineola, New York

## *DEDICATION*

*To my aunt, Arlene Mothes Anderson,*
*whose love of flowers and gardens has*
*always been an inspiration to me.*

## NOTE

Popularized by Pierre-Joseph Redouté (1759–1840), who produced volumes of delicate, highly detailed flowers, plant and floral illustration peaked in the period between the early 18th and late 19th centuries. These rare collections of hand-colored engravings attempted to combine scientific accuracy with aesthetic appeal. As a record of natural history, these flower prints often depicted new botanical species. English botanist Joseph Dalton Hooker (1817–1911) was one such artist, traveling to the Antarctic and making many botanical discoveries.

Flower lovers and botanists will be enamored of these exquisite black-and-white renderings of beautiful blooms. Captions include the flower's common name and scientific name, as well as the illustrator of the original print. All thirty flower prints are shown in color on the inside covers.

*Bibliographical Note*

*Color Your Own Great Flower Prints* is a new work, first published by Dover Publications, Inc., in 2001.

DOVER *Pictorial Archive* SERIES

*International Standard Book Number: 0-486-41553-8*

Manufactured in the United States of America
Dover Publications, Inc., 31 East 2nd Street, Mineola, N.Y. 11501

1. Vase of Flowers, from an original illustration by Tessier.

2. Study of Flowers, from an original illustration by Roubillac.

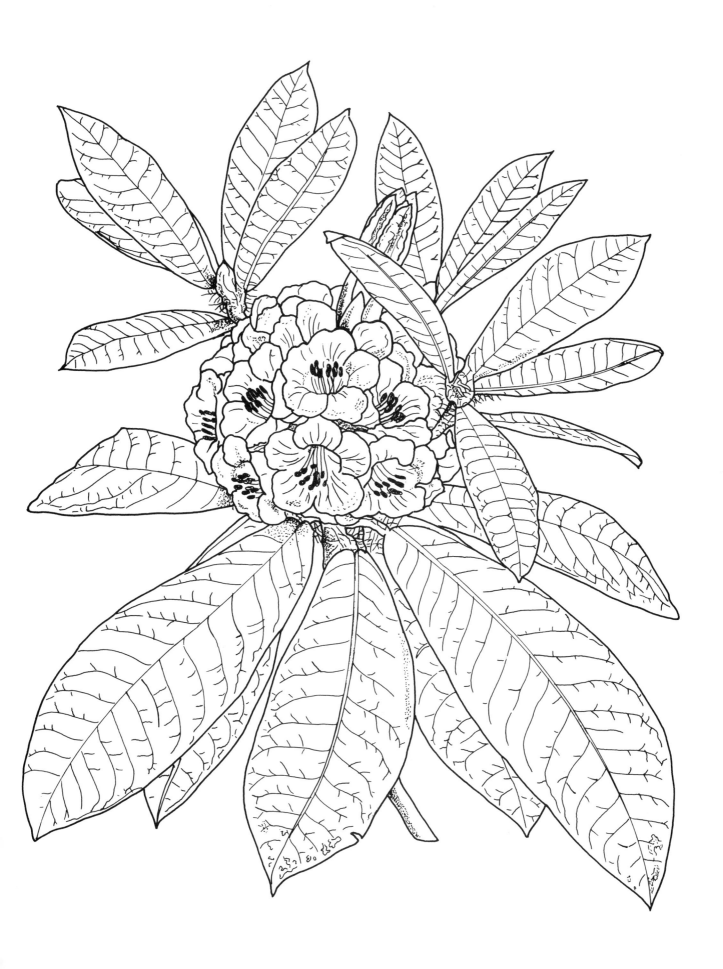

3. Bristly rhododendron *(Rhododendron barbatum),* from an original illustration
by Joseph Dalton Hooker.

4. Orris, iris *(Iris pallida),* from an original illustration by Pierre-Joseph Redouté.

5. Fancy pansies (*Viola* species), from an original illustration
by Worthington George Smith.

6. Hollyhock *(Alcea rosea)*, from an original illustration by Jean Louis Prévost.

7. Canterbury bells *(Campanula medium)*, from an original illustration
by Pierre-Joseph Redouté.

8. Egyptian lotus, blue lotus *(Nymphaea caerulea),* from an original illustration by Pierre-Joseph Redouté.

9. Collection of Flowers, from an original illustration by Jean Louis Prévost.

10. Bird-of-paradise flower *(Strelitzia reginae),* from an original illustration by Francis Bauer.

11. Orchids *(Epidendrum vitellinum)*, from an original illustration by Miss Drake.

12. Orchids *(Cattleya percivaliana)*, from an original illustration by Henry Sanders.

13. Frangipani *(Plumeria rubra)*, from an original illustration by Georg Dionysus Ehret.

14. Magnolia *(Magnolia campbellii),* from an original illustration by Joseph Dalton Hooker.

15. Camellia, Japan rose *(Camellia japonica),* from an original illustration by Clara Maria Pope.

16. French rose *(Rosa gallica versicolor),* from an original illustration
by Pierre-Joseph Redouté.

17. Austrian brier rose (*Rosa foetida,* var, Bicolor), from an original illustration by Alfred Parsons.

18. Tree peony *(Paeonia moutan, Paeonia suffruticosa)*, from an original illustration by Pierre-Joseph Redouté.

19. Peony (*Paeonia* species), from an original illustration by Pierre Buc'hoz.

20. Peonies *(Paeonia officinalis)*, from an original illustration by Johann Jakob Walther.

21. American Turk's-cap lily *(Lilium superbum)*, from an original illustration by Georg Dionysus Ehret.

22. Orange lily *(Lilium bulbiferum)*, from an original illustration by John Edwards.

23. Showy lily, Japanese lily *(Lilium speciosum),* from an original illustration by Walter Fitch.

24. Amaryllis *(Amaryllis equestris major)*, from an original illustration by Mrs. E. Bury.

25. Sunflower (*Helianthus* species), from an original illustration by John Miller.

26. Varieties of the Auricula *(Primula auricula)*, from an original illustration
by John Edwards.

27. Tulips (*Tulipa* species), from an original illustration by John Edwards.

28. Parrot tulip *(Tulipa gesneriana)*, from an original illustration by Georg Dionysus Ehret.

29. Imperial gloriosa, glory lily (*Gloriosa* species), from an original illustration by John Hill.

30. Madeira foxglove *(Digitalis sceptrum)*, from an original illustration
by Ferdinand Lukas Bauer.